EARSHOT

EARSHOT

Morris Panych

Talonbooks

2001

Talonbooks
P.O. Box 2076, Vancouver, British Columbia, Canada V6B 3S3
www.talonbooks.com

Typeset in Scala and printed and bound in Canada by Hignell Book
Printing.

First Printing: April 2001

National Library of Canada Cataloguing in Publication Data

Panych, Morris.
  Earshot

  A play.
  ISBN 0-88922-444-7

  I. Title.
PS8581.A65E27 2001   C812'.54   C2001-910193-7
PR9199.3.P325E27 2001

The publisher gratefully acknowledges the financial support of the
Canada Council for the Arts; the Government of Canada through the
Book Publishing Industry Development Program; and the Province of
British Columbia through the British Columbia Arts Council for our
publishing activities.

Earshot was first produced by Tarragon Theatre in Toronto on February 13, 2001 with the following cast and crew:

DOYLE: Randy Hughson

Directed by Morris Panych
Set and Costumes designed by Ken MacDonald
Lighting designed by John Thompson
Sound designed by Derek Bruce
Stage Manager: Gretel Meyer Odell

The photographs on pages 14, 28, 46 and 57 are of Randy Hughson starring in the première Tarragon Theatre production of Earshot. *Photographs by Cylla von Tiedemann.*

Prologue/

Dawn. A dirty little room in forced perspective. From below, street sounds. Music begins. As it plays, noise from other apartments is heard, serendipitously following the beat — telephones, typewriters, flushing toilets — until the fully orchestrated sounds of the neighbours play together like a symphony. The room fades to black. Music continues then stops.

1/

*Doyle stands in the middle of the room,
holding a brown paper package, sporting
industrial strength protective ear-mufflers,
inside of which he wears a set of earplugs,
inside of which, wads of cotton are stuffed.*

DOYLE
I'm back, everyone. Not to worry.

*He removes the paraphernalia. An alarm
clock rings next door. He places the package
on the table as the alarm continues; talks to
one wall as he points to the other.*

Well, gee, Mrs. Noon. I wonder who was out half
the night again.

Goes over the the wall. Listens.

Valerie?

*He sighs. Hits the wall with his fist. Alarm
stops.*

Aspirin is above the sink.

*He sits on the bed, leaning his head on the
wall. Blackout.*

2/

*Doyle sits in his underwear, composing a
letter.*

DOYLE
My dearest neighbour. My darling — my dear —
my dear darling — my —

He writes.

Valerie. As you read this — as you read this —
this — this — this —

Jackhammers in the distance.

Will there ever be enough holes in the world?

Keys lock a door. He stops.

As you — There. See? Puts the key in her coat
pocket. Then opens her purse to put the key
away. What would you call that? Said hello, once,
then answered the phone.

Footsteps. Stopping.

Ever since she moved from across the hall, seems
perpetually turned around. Aphasia, I think.

Footsteps turn and limp off the other way.

Poor Valerie.

At the letter again.

What have we got so far? As you read this —
this —

Drifts off for a moment.

Yes, it's true. I'm sitting here in my, in my
underpants. Unmoved, once again, by the clarion
call of industry, Mrs. Noon. Idle — for another
day. But perhaps only for another day. Depending
on the — on the —

The truth is, I don't have the inspiration this
morning to wear trousers. I went out the day
before yesterday, and that was — someone needs
a new blade in that razor — was quite enough
thank you. Let's just say, the effort it takes to
continually reaffirm my status as an
unemployable mental case — too much
competition in the oddball field, sorry. Even the
case worker is nuttier than — I am. Smells
strangely of disinfectant, talks through the fingers
of her right hand like it was a — what —
intercom; and has never once — honestly, looked
up at me. Not once. Well, obviously it would
destroy the delicate take-a-number-and-I'll-be-
right-with-you relationship we've built up over
the months. Besides, it was a very big day for me,
as I mentioned. Did I mention? Momentous. A
'paradigm shift', as the au courant like to say.
Well, I don't know if it's the au courant, Mrs.
Noon. Somebody likes to say it; it isn't me. I don't
like the word 'shift' for one thing, it reminds me
of my former night desk duties; as for
'paradigms' — that just sounds like twenty cents

to me. Ha, ha. But for emphasis, I'll use the phrase — if only for emphasis. A paradigm shift in my thinking. It has nothing, of course, *whatsoever*, to do with my current state of undress. Or maybe it does. That the direction of my life has changed is perhaps, who knows, an understatement.

Oh , stop it, Mrs. Noon. For God sakes, please. He's not — he's — how many times do we have to — would you listen to it?! 'Harold? Harold?' Christ. Harold is dead. *Dead*, you nit wit. Got it? It's just me; your — you know — your unfortunate next door — Harold wheezed his last wheeze and he — (*distracted by a sound*)

Is that what you think it's about? Unrequited love? Well, that's — just —

How little you know me, my dear.

Such a nice, old-fashioned, word for such a — 'unrequited' — for such a — don't you think? Why not *decapitated* love? Or *heart-ripped-from-your-chest-still-beating-and-thrown-into-a-burning-river* love. How about *guts-pulled-out-and wrapped-in-a-parcel-and-mailed-with-insufficient-postage-to-the-Arctic-circle* —

A sudden calm.

In fact, why call it 'love'?

Harold can't hear you. Harold is —

I passed by a Chinese funeral the other — did I tell you? Fireworks. If you can believe it.

When I was thirteen I fell head over heels with this character in a movie. Talk about unrequited. To this day I can't eat any amount of stale buttered popcorn without feeling this stabbing chest — hiatal hernia, they say, but just in case, I've given up going to films as a pastime. Besides, if I really needed to have people sit directly behind me and free-associate for two hours, I could ride a bus.

Not that I — public transit would be fine if it wasn't quite so — what's the — ? So public. I don't mean the inane conversation; that goes without saying. It's the incidental noise that clatters so unbearably in my ears. The jangling of cheap jewellry, the rattling of old men, the crackling of chewing gum. Humanity. What an excruciating burble. Why haven't I stabbed myself in the side of the head, yet, with a letter opener? Well, that's an excellent question. I'll tell you why; aside from having a letter opener of any real quality. Because up until now — up until — let's say yesterday — despite my freakish auditory — *sensitivity* — I was actually spared the sound of my own thoughts. I say despite, but what I really mean is *because* of. The racket. In my — you know — this thing.

Hits the side of his head.

Of course, no, you have no idea what I'm talking about. You don't even know what's going on in your own apartment, let alone mine. Tapping your tap, tap, tap, cane, through all that bric-a-brac, chattering to a man who *passed away two weeks ago* if only you could remember. All that gasping; please; the clutching, the gurgling. If we'd called emergency, of course, you're right. But you know what they're like; all those sirens. One cardiac arrest and it's Armageddon. Besides, you can't really *find* your telephone, can you? And I don't like to use mine — just in — you know — in case. I mean, for example, the telephone survey people called here just the other day; to ask my opinion of telephone surveys.

What's not to like? Good God. Someone's actually — can you believe it? — listening.

And anyway. It's been peace and quiet from Harold ever since. An end to his endless expectorating; so redolent it was it used to make me produce my own phlegm. Anyway, he's dead, and that's more or less the end of it.

One does wonder, though, when you're finally going to get around to having him — you know — taken away.

as you read this — as you read *this* — you will hear a — hear a — does a gun pop, or does it bang?

Typing above. He sighs. Writes.

3/

*Late night. Doyle listens at the wall,
following the scene next door at Valerie's, as
she arrives home, alone. He listens, touching
the wall with his hands, then pressing his
whole body against it. He presses and presses,
breathing it in. Blackout.*

4/

Another day. Doyle sits on his bed, licking an envelope.

DOYLE
There she is at the china again.

Abruptly sitting up.

It's the cheap clatter of it. If it wasn't so — hollow and completely —

Too late. There. I've stamped it. See? It's out of my — it's — stamped. It's addressed and it's stamped. So there you are. Good as done.

What are you sorting? It's a side-plate, a side-plate! Now you've done it. Smash!! All over the — that's right. Just — stand there, stupidly looking down at all the broken bits. How, eh? How does it all end up in those little broken bits? See if you can't step on them, now. Grind them under foot. That's it. Why not have a go at the cups, while you're at it. So this is what happens in the end. Everything just slips out of your hands. Before you know it, you're diapered and dumbfounded, shuffling from room to room; slippers slippering along the floor like a couple of old — ragmops; cane tapping in time; tap, shuffle, shuffle, tap, shuffle, shuffle, like a never-ending geriatric soft shoe routine. Stopping for a moment, now and again, to try and get your husband's attention.

Having no more luck now than when he was
alive.

Toilet flushing.

Mr. Rasky and his toilet again. We're in for
another long day, everyone. An obsessive-
compulsive with an intestinal disorder makes for
a lot of extra flushing.

Knock next door.

I don't believe it.

Doyle bounds over to the wall.

There's knocking at your door, Mrs. Noon. Not a
slight knock. Not the small single-knuckled,
polite knock of inquiry from a concerned
neighbour or some hapless girl guide; no. It's the
brutish, perfunctory thud of dispatch.

I wonder who's called Social Services.

Blackout.

5/

Later. Music next door.

DOYLE
Why didn't they take you both away? Save a trip
to the morgue. To what *indefinite* end, one loathes
to ask, can you wander aimlessly through that
wasteland of antimacassars and porcelain
ballerinas, in search of the old goat. Calling out to
each empty room, with your mouthful of missing
teeth. *They've taken him away.*

There goes the mailman. Of course I only mailed
it — was it yesterday? Tomorrow, everyone.

He puts the package under the bed.

Where are your dentures, by the way? Where did
they get to? Why don't I give you a hint. Try the
top of the fridge where you left them last *July*. Or
can't you hear them vibrating against the glass,
on and off, at regular intervals? All — throughout
— the *night*. Of course, if you can't even hear
your mantle clock — with its ever-so-slightly
irregular rhythm. Actually stopping, now and
then, altogether. A clock with its own sense of
time. As if the world wasn't ironic enough.

Noise above.

And then of course at the other end of the
spectrum there's Plimley.

Listens.

It isn't so much that you occupy that wheelchair, Plimley. It's the way you occupy it. Did I say occupy? Stress, is the thing. Pressing down on the rubber, with such a furious emphasis, such a — listen to that.

Only a matter of time before he comes through the ceiling.

Ceiling creaks.

It's as if he's always trying to make a point, isn't it? With every nasty little turn of the wheel. I'm *handicapped!* All that huffing and puffing; sighing — the demonstrative dropping of things — we couldn't feel more sorry for you if we tried. Especially Valerie. But that's just not good enough, is it Mrs. Noon? No. Our pity isn't sop enough for him. Won't even answer the door when she brings him fresh baking. My God, I'd cut off both my legs for just a *whiff* of that dessert. And if you think that's an exaggeration, Plimley, then you don't know me very well. In fact, you don't know me at all, but if you did, you'd realize just how wrong you'd be to assume that I wouldn't smash my own *head* through the wall if she asked me to. Of course she wouldn't. That's the point, isn't it? That's the — she doesn't expect people to do things for her. To wait on her hand and foot. Then turn around and show their true feelings for the world, like someone we know, by not even bothering to answer the fucking door. Snapping out the lights! Sitting there in the dark, breathing contempt through

his reedy nostrils. And with her self-esteem
problems.

Beat.

On her feet all day long, poor creature, with her
customers and their dermatological complaints;
limping home in those ill-fitting — you can hear
her all the way down the street — clip, ouch, clop,
ouch, to spend one *entire* evening squishing
blueberries and oatmeal into a pan. I thought she
was laying the foundation for a small *building* in
there. Nearly missed a whole night of desperate
bar-hopping in the process. Not that she needs to
go out anymore than she — my God, the
woman's appetite for social self-abuse is
insatiable and that's no secret.

Typing continues.

Go ahead and ignore me; just rattle away on your
nasty little typewriter. Completely dejected, she
was. Slinking back down into her apartment, and
sitting there, picking and munching her way
through an entire blueberry crumble, until
neither of us could take it anymore. Is it any
wonder I pulled the fire alarm? But don't listen to
a word I have to say. Not that you were anyway,
but if you were I'd have to say — I'd definitely
have to say 'pay no attention, Plimley.' Pay no
attention to any of us at all.

Beat. Listens. Typing continues.

The wounded everyman in his garret. Tuned in to public radio broadcasts, and as if that isn't pretentious enough — Christ — smoking a pipe? Who smokes a pipe these days? Except some idiot in a play. In lieu of a character. Most other people manage their self absorption without actually making a hollow sucking sound. Isn't that right, Mrs. — Mrs. —

Beat.

I know you're sleeping in there, dear. No city garbage truck idles for that long. Then again, she's up all night. Wearing out that poor old 78 record. Drifting through the dust and broken china. As if there's one more thing left to do; if only she could remember, 'Oh, right. I forgot to expire'.

Listens.

Harold did everything, is the problem. Even fed her. How does she sustain herself now, one asks, in his absence? Saltines, naturally. The masticating is *epic*, in a word. That the woman lives entirely on crackers, Plimley, aside from being a source of unendurable mulching for the rest of us, is of some nutritional concern. If she can survive on those alone, she may never perish. I don't cite this as a reason for my fateful decision, of course. Don't forget. I survived her husband and his diseases of the bowels. There was a rumpus.

It wasn't the greatest of his assaults, either. Who can forget the bladder that drained like an eyedropper. I've never been so incontinent in my life. But I've lived through worse. Through a lifetime of unimaginable ... racket.

Beat.

Who knows; this might have gone on forever, this hearing things to the extent I — do. If not for — for —

Beat.

I want it to be a definite —

A finger to his head.

— statement, you know. I don't want Valerie to dismiss it. That's the thing. I couldn't bear that. I want her to be moved by my act. On some — level, I want her to be — she will. She'll be moved.

There'll be a discussion in the hallway, at the very least. Guns don't go off every day. She'll wonder at least.

She'll — ice cream truck; you see? She'll begin to construct a picture of me in her mind. It's my only way in, frankly, my — to her thoughts. Risky, of course. She may just think putting a bullet through my head was simply a — an act of — you know.

Suicide.

He never sells any ice cream. Just goes round and round the block as if to make a point.

Of course I've explained all this in the — in the
— that's why I — Why did I write a letter? I'm
not a — I think I misspelled 'fait accompli' —
Plimley's the writer around here. He certainly has
the rejections to prove it.

What was I thinking? What was I — too late. Too
late. Gone. Good.

Fixes some tea. Stops.

I cherish that moment; don't you? When he gets
his little envelope from some publisher. The faith
of that — God — that moment almost
replenishes the soul, Mrs Noon. As he eagerly
worms and wriggles his finger under the flap,
slowly pushing, little by little, at the opening.
Even though he knows, still he hopes. He *hopes*.
Sliding the letter out as if the contents might
change his life forever. Exalt him from this
purgatory. But no, he can't read it, yet. No. He
rinses out his souvenir tumbler. The thinness of
the glass, unmistakable; that slight gritty abrasion
of the shaky hand, wrapping itself around the
embossed insignia of some long-forgotten
promotional gimmick. Then into the bottom
dribbles that little finger of scotch. We know the
sound of that cheap scotch, don't we. Poured with
all the breathless attention of a scientist and his
uranium.

I almost come to feel sorry for him.

As the paper leaves his hand after he reads it;
drops, like a fallen angel, and plummets to the
floor. To lie there, with the rest of its comrades,
carpeting his unsuccessful career. Biscuit?

These are a little past their 'best before' date. But that could be said about most of us.

Clack, clack, clack, clack, clack, clack, clack, clack. Type your head off, Mr. Plimley.

I wonder if that could happen.

Off a sound.

Someone's chewing something; what is that horrific — ? It's me. Never mind. Emergency over, Mrs. Noon.

It was important she not think of me not as a dead person, slumped in the corner, his brains dripping, linguini carbonara-like, down the wall, but as something essential. A reverberation. Through the halls. This disparate and useless life, suddenly crystallized into the single — resolute — pop — of a gun. A parting shot.

Like those Chinese mourners, over in the — as I — in the — letting off rockets and pinwheels for some dead relative; and, who knows, perhaps because the sun was coming up, but it suddenly dawned on me, ha ha. This is right. This is how it should end. Bang. And a bit of smoke drifting up into the morning air.

Somewhere, a toilet flushes.

In the end what are words? A gunshot, I think, speaks for itself.

Blackout.

6/

*Typing above. The sounds of a t.v. next door
at Valerie's. Doyle lies about, reading a book
on weaponry.*

DOYLE
She has a habit, sometimes, of turning the t.v. on
instead of off when she goes out. Soap operas.
The first week she lived here, I thought she had a
brain tumour and two weeks to live. Not to
mention an apartment full of callous, baritoned
doctors.

The only person who's ever visited her was that
— what-do-you-call-it — amputee she brought
home from the Veterans Club. An embarrassing
night for everyone.

A man has to be in an awful big hurry, to leave
and forget his leg.

A plate smashes.

And there was the Lutheran minister — with the
lisp; that's right. Have we ever been forced to sit
through such — a salivating dinner conversation,
Mrs. Noon? How could anyone so dry be so wet?
Sputtering on about religious doctrine on the one
hand, while slipping the other hand under her
crinkly cotton blouse.

Thank God for those sudden, mysterious strains
of the Bach 'Passion'

Blowing dust off an album.

In the distance.

Which he correctly interpreted as divine intervention.

Didn't even close the door behind him. Men. Left a broken heart and a blueberry crumble.

He plays Bach.

She thought about him for weeks. Not a day passed when she didn't hurry home to sit by the phone, tapping her nails. I nearly went mad. Her stubby eyebrow pencil circling each passing day in the calendar. Little idiot.

If I didn't love her so much, I think I'd hate her. You see what an impossible situation I'm in? Why don't I just go ahead and shoot myself? What more do I need? Besides a gun. I mean a proper one.

Wrenching the recording from the player.

This stupid country and its stupid gun laws. There's something — I'm sorry — not quite right about having to kill yourself with an antique. I'm perfectly capable of handling an everyday weapon, thank you, and I think my psychiatric evaluation can back me up. How many beer-swilling moosehunters can make that claim? Eh, Mrs. Noon? In those hats? Like our friend, downstairs.

Where is he anyway? Would a hunting accident
be too much to hope for?

Keys in a door.

No. I don't believe it. He's back.

Door opens, footsteps

It can't be. No sooner do I mention the bastard —
God help us.
It's the whistler!

Whistling below.

Never mind. I've got a gun.

All I need, now, is a flint, some black powder and
a muzzle loader.

Blackout.

7/

Whistling.

DOYLE

Listen. Just — he meanders. There's no point to it. It doesn't relate to any discernible melody at all. I used to wonder, 'Is that Wagner whistled badly or Schoenberg whistled well?' But, no. It's not anything at all. Just — it's noise. Shrill, air-rending noise. No purpose to it; no direction at all but to invade silence.

Whistling continues.

Things had been so sombre of late. Now he's back to lighten the mood. And the thing is, the thing is — you see — he's not happy. That's the worst of it, Remple.

Tossing the cushions.

Why would you need to assert it in such ear-splitting fashion if you were? It's a cover, and we know what for. Isn't that right, Mrs. —

Beat.

Oh, God. What's she doing now?

Phone ringing somewhere.

Thank you for reminding me; I need to cancel my phone service. For one thing, it avoids that awkward bill-arriving-after-the-suicide situation that we all hate, and for another thing, I would've had to anyway. I no longer have the funds.

They cut me off, the bastards. Did you know that, Plimley? They're on to me at the welfare office. Oh, yes. They think I'm employable. Isn't that — I suppose if you include preoccupation as an occupation. They don't know what kind of contribution I'm making to the economy at present, by staying well out of it. The last job I had, I caused a lot of trouble and embarrassment for everyone and that's the truth. Security firm! How about an insecurity firm? If you've ever worked in a museum at night you have only one question.

Why don't they find better glue for those dinosaurs?

It's just the tip of the iceberg, you know, all this putting of people to work, Plimley. If they have their way, the fears of German expressionists everywhere will be realized.

A horrible thought.

I should have got myself back on welfare before I did this. Before I — otherwise everybody is going to naturally just assume that I killed myself because of my — you know — *financial* — I might even become a rallying point of some kind. Posthumous hero of social reform, is what I don't want to be. Martyr of liberals. It wouldn't be right, Plimley. I don't actually support welfare, as it happens. I just, you know — collect it.

Don't mention that to Valerie, by the way. After the fact. When you're all gathered in the hallway, watching them apply the strips of yellow police tape to my door. She'd only think I was a prick, if she knew. Maybe she should. It gives me some edge. Otherwise, what was I? Ambience? Frankly, I can't decide. Is it better for people to have a bad opinion about you, or no opinion at all? In the end? There it is, you see. The dilemma faced everyday by publicists and assassins alike.

Beat of concern.

He's stopped whistling, that's a bad sign. Only so many reasons, none of them good, for interrupting that screeching cacophony. Eating is one, but even then — I heard him — honestly — try, once, to whistle his way through a mouthful of — I'm pretty sure — Polish sausage. Thinking is the other. Dreaming up his next do-it-yourself adventure.

Tapping below.

God help us — he's not moving that picture again. Now he'll have to spackle and sand over the old spot.

Reflecting.

Remember when he used to have an actual job? Those were the days, eh. A longshoreman, we assumed, since he was often out on strike, but still he was engaged in an outside activity. But then they went and retired him because of the — you know — *incident,* and it's never been the same.

Well yes, it's true — for years, I had to wake with his five-thirty alarm every morning and suffer through those interminable crunchy breakfasts. That long, operatic shower, those chipper little razor strokes. The shocking toilet bowl declarations. But at least he was out by seven. The place fell silent, at last, except for the dripping hot water faucet.

You can always tell it's hot, of course, the way it keens a little inside the pipes.

We were free of him at any rate. For the whole day. Until a few months ago, wasn't it? Perhaps only a few weeks, I don't know. When his little home projects began in earnest. The sudden frantic re-hinging of the kitchen cupboard doors? The meticulous stripping and sanding of baseboards? The counting of his entire penny collection? Twice. Oh, yes. The re-sorting of the spice rack; that was — he only has six spices, and it took a day and a half. And let's not forget the endless daily pacing, as he scouts the apartment for something more to get his hands on. But, really, it's the relocating of this picture that gets to me. Every time he moves the stupid thing, he has to rearrange all the furniture around it. I can tell by where he puts the lamp, that it's not a thing he wants to look at. In fact, it's something he wants to avoid. So why does he keep it? Old habit? Obligation, perhaps? Superstition? A photograph, possibly, since a painting would hardly illicit such a personal response. Someone close to him certainly, but who? Gazing out, accusatorially, from inside the frame. Who is it, then, Remple? That you don't even know you're afraid of, eh?

Beat.

I'll tell you when I first realized it was a mirror. Remember how you always used to stop in front of it every morning, if only for a brief moment, before you went out to work? Now, you no longer stop at all. Can't face your utter redundancy, Remple. Don't realize you're doing it, of course. You're happier than ever, as far as your concerned. Got your whole life ahead of you; to putter away at.

Busy as ever. Back from your — whatever, trip through the local marshes if those squishy boots are anything to go by. Bagged a couple of unsuspecting quail by the sound of it. Unless those are your own intestines that just slid out into the sink. You never eat the bloody things, do you. Gut them, wrap them up; a year later chip them out of the back of the freezer and toss them away. That sort of sound isn't easy to decipher, I'll have you know. A frozen quail carcass hitting the bottom of a metal waste basket at four in the morning is in a category all its own.

Blackout.

8/

He sits with package. Listens intently.

DOYLE
> Over to the mailbox. Jiggles that tiny key into that
> tiny lock. Jiggle. Jiggle. Wait. Remple whistles
> past her, on his way out to the hardware store.
> She pauses. Right. He's gone. Mailbox opens,
> with that familiar squeak; voilà — single
> envelope. Slides it out.
>
> Cellophane window.
>
> Bill.
>
> *Returns the package beneath his bed.*
>
> Where is that letter? I'll be having second
> thoughts, next. No I won't.
>
> It hurts my feet to hear her climb the stairs;
> Christ. Especially in those shoes. She won't think
> of taking the easy way up.
>
> Too considerate to use the elevator. Never know
> when some paraplegic typist might need a quick
> ride down to the liquor store for inspiration. Did
> I say quick? There's no contraption slower that
> isn't actually run by hamsters on fly-wheels.
>
> And does he pay attention to the 'out of service'
> sign; so clearly posted?
>
> I'm going to have to think of something else.

Looking for her keys, of course. Stops when she gets to the door; the wrong door. Goes through that whole purse. They're where she put them. Always in the left pocket. Poor thing.

The mind. What a contraption.

In her purse, is a plastic button, which fell off the sleeve of her coat, once, and bounced down the stairs, to the landing. She picked it up, and popped it in her purse. So now, as soon as she finds the button, she remembers how it fell off the coat, and as soon as she thinks of the coat, the remembers the keys. Poor thing. If she ever sews the button back on that coat, she'll never find her keys again.

And that's what makes me love her, Mrs. Noon.

That and the sound of her legs rubbing together as she walks.

Blackout.

9/

Later. Lights up on Doyle, sitting in a chair,
his ear pressed to the wall.

DOYLE
Slowly. No; slowly. Let it just — no. *Slip,*
diaphanously. Honest to Christ. You let that wool
skirt of yours drop like a dirty laundry bag,
Valerie. Can't you just tease me a little? The
bathwater's too hot, anyway. What's your rush,
for God's sake? There will always be men,
waiting in bars, anxious to pay you no attention.
It's what men do. No; don't put anything on just
yet. Let me admire the small of your back for just
a little — ugh — I wish the stupid robe was at the
very least silk. If I had the money — I don't like
the way terrytowel grabs at your, at your — not
that I blame it. At your skin. I'm just, just
jealous, that's all. I'm jealous of your robe.

You see how you make me say the stupidest
things?

As he slips a hand down his pants. Suddenly.

Honest to goodness, Mrs. Noon! Shut — up.

Nothing turns a person off like senile dementia.

Terrycloth doesn't suit you. Only the highest
quality of everything. It's what your skin
deserves. I've never heard such lovely skin. Even

against the obscene lacerations of polyester and — viscose.

Sawing below.

What's he doing, now? If I had any concentration at all, these people would have thrown it right out the window.

The pantyhose, yes. That's it, that's it. Your lovely derrière slipping out, like, like — oh God. Two — poached — half-peaches? No; I diminish it with commentary. The sound, the sound of your little bum. Is there anything in words to describe it? Don't peel off the legs so quickly. The nylon against your leg stubble is all I live for.

Did I say 'live'? God. Wait, the water's still too hot, Valerie. Don't — there. What did I tell you? You always pour it too hot, because you underestimate the delicacy of your skin. Not me. I would never do that. I would wash your back with a sponge so soft it probably wouldn't even be a sponge. It would probably just be the word 'sponge', whispered over your shoulders. Like the breeze on a lake.

Mrs. Noon. Is that you eating, or is someone slapping a thick coat of paint on the walls with a raw piece of liver?

The thing is, you see, the truth of it is, I could never touch you with anything but the softest softness of my voice. This flesh is too coarse. This body too abrasive; with its hair and its elbows and its — its — No. I don't think you'd find me very pleasant company at all. To start with, I'm — well, I'm human. And you deserve better. And of course, I have this hearing — thing. This problem. As you know. Not that I have a problem hearing. It's a problem, as you know, of hearing too much; which is really much more of a problem, as you know, than not hearing at all. Not deafness; *deafening*.

It was a kind of deafness at first. As an infant, I had tinnitus so extreme no other sound could penetrate.

Sighs. Hammering below.

One can only hope he's building his own coffin down there.

Beat.

The ear-ringing condition suited me fine. I had no interest in the outside world. But fed up with my circumspection, and no doubt annoyed by my blissful indifference, my mother dragged me off to some dingy office above a button shop one day, where I was ushered behind a beaded curtain, by this blind Uzbeki woman; her thin cold fingers gripping the back of my neck. Everything smelled of tar. They had to hold my head down. The pain was — what's worse than unimaginable? And for what, Valerie? To become a freak of nature? To spend the rest of my days hearing a pin drop. Did I say 'drop'? I can hear it *dropping*.

Beat.

My mother wanted me cured. What good was a child who not only wouldn't listen; couldn't listen? Who would she complain to about her swollen feet? Or order about like a servant; send out for cigarettes and petroleum jelly.

Whatever they poured into my ears, it worked; if their intention was to turn life into a nightmare. The ringing stopped; my ears were opened.

But did I need to know there were termites inside the walls? When you can hear the blood coursing through your veins, Valerie, you can hear too much. There are things, believe me, that a ten-year-old just doesn't need to be exposed to. I knew, for instance, that my mother had men over, now and again. But I never knew, until then, what her fingernails sounded like, digging into their bare, writhing backs. The world opened up like a big, giant, blaring trumpet and blasted me with its horrors. The clamour of people, everywhere, weeping, suffocating, ordering their french fries. What do you listen to, Valerie, when you can hear everything?

At the heating vent.

Remple's nightly confessions? They're still scraping that buddy of his off the bottom of the shipping crate.

Beat.

Don't go out tonight, Valerie.

Head leaning on the wall.

Your water's ready by the way. I know exactly
what the temperature is because the pipes tell
me. Just as I can hear how much bubble bath you
pour; thankfully enough that it crinkles all
around your body; describing to me the exact
shape of you from top to bottom. Everything
around you conspires to give you away, Valerie,
without your even knowing it. Your plastic
bracelets, your secret stash of almond crunch, the
onion-skin of your King James Bible — in which
you meditate a little too long, if my hearing is
right, on the lusty bits in Solomon; your patient
devotion to television doctors, let's not forget. The
unremovable blueberry stains on your sofa. That
mysterious page in your high school annual. Is it
the young man you always call out for in your
dreams, rolling over to embrace him, and hitting
the wall? And, of course, there are those nightly
backstage preparations for what we'll call the
tragi-comedy of your love life. Somebody had to
say it.

You really are an actress. Makeup, costume.
Becoming your character, the way I suppose an
actress must, without the least anticipation of the
evening's calamitous, and drunken conclusion —
in order to play your part to its fullest. Enter
Valerie. Returning, alone. Stumbling up the stair.
Diligently threading the key into the lock. The
wrong lock at first, but never mind. Turning
yourself around and falling headlong through the
apartment. Landing like a sack of stones on your
griping old brass bed.

I could sit up the whole night, listening to its
creaks and complaints. Follow those rusty

contours. Shaping your hips and your shoulders.
If I was right beside you, I couldn't be as close.

In a way, thank God for this vast chasm of inches.
This drywall, and these studs.

I'd rather have been a distant thought, in the end.
A lingering doubt — like smoke from a gun.
Bang! Pop! Either way. A loud question,
reverberating in your mind. 'What was that?' At
least I'd be on your mind.

After all, if you saw me on the street, you
certainly wouldn't know I existed. And don't say
you would — don't — because I already know the
truth. Don't be angry with me, but who do you
think the untidy-looking gentleman was, standing
on the other side of the counter the other day,
asking improbably about moisturizers? Did he
really seem like the moisturizer type to you?

Forgive me.

I couldn't bear it any longer.

I hoped against hope that something might
happen, then and there. Aside from a lashing of
face-cream. I should have learned from Plimley,
by now. Rejection? Inevitable I don't know what I
was — what was I — ? That you might like me?
To your credit, you didn't. You acted in a
completely professional manner, I have to say.
Although that toner was a little on the abrasive
side. As we discussed my complexion, it was
sweet of you not to shiver with revulsion. And
anyway, what else should we talk about? I
suppose I thought you might find me, in some
way — I don't know — moderately engaging?

Something. No. You served me like I was a —
customer. I know. I long ago made an agreement
with myself. Never to make myself known to you.
But what a terrible day for me, Valerie. They
booted me off welfare. Can you think of anything
more ignominious? A drug trafficker with a
refugee hearing can do better. It suddenly
occurred to me: I don't exist. They were the only
people who actually knew I was alive.

I found myself kicking helplessly, aimlessly
through the streets.

I know where you work because every time they
advertise on t.v., you sing along with the jingle.
You're so uncommonly loyal.

Offering candy.

It's Almond Roca. Your favorite.

I shouldn't have gone; but what would promises
be if you kept them?

I needed a friend, not a — you know — facial.
That's when I realized the truth. The only thing
there will ever be between us, is a wall.

Off the other wall.

Oh, *Harold, Harold, Harold, Harold.*

> *More typing. Fade to black as he offers
> almond roca to the wall, then eats one.*

10/

*Morning. Doyle lies on his bed, talking to
Mrs. Noon.*

DOYLE
Is there anything left in that apartment, Mrs.
Noon, that hasn't been — ?

A plate smashes.

Elevator.

Poor Plimley. Off he goes, once again. Clutching
a greasy brown submission envelope between his
sweaty knees. Wheeling down to the corner for
his stamps; the first mistake. How much faith, a
publisher can't help but wonder, does a writer
have in his own work, to place it in the hands of
the Post Office? But there it is. Perhaps faith isn't
it. Perhaps he's found a kind of spiritual peace in
the gesture itself. The Zen of The Unsolicited
Manuscript.

Listens to Mrs. Noon.

Spoons. What's she doing with spoons?

Whistling below. Doyle goes to his sink.

There. Back from his morning stroll. What could
be worse. The sun shining, the birds chirping; a
whole day of puttering ahead.

Shower below.

And nothing, whatsoever, to put a damper on his day. Except a sudden shortage of hot water.

Doyle turns a tap.

Or maybe a sudden scalding.

Doyle switches taps. Shouts below. Ignoring them, he runs over to the wall and listens.

Taking another day off? That's two this month. Valerie?

Beat.

She's ignoring me. I should never have put in that appearance. Did I learn nothing from Victor Hugo? Anyway, there won't be anymore of it, Valerie, you can be assured of that. You'll be happy to know I have a definite plan of action. I can't say what it is, you'll have to wait for the postal service.

You don't look after yourself, you know. You need more than —

Listens.

— seltzer for breakfast.

You really should be in bed with that headache. The brandy wasn't enough, was it? You had to get into the peppermint schnapps again. And no one to hold your head over the toilet bowl once again. Why do you do it — darling?

Whistling below.

What can I do to make him stop?

He gets down and listens at the hot air vent.

What's he — would you like to know what he's
doing at the moment? He's opening and shutting
a drawer. Over and over. Over and over. He opens
it, he shuts it, he opens it, he shuts it. Opens,
shuts, opens, shuts. One thing's clear. It opens
and shuts perfectly. So obviously he'll be fixing
that next.

Doyle stands and jumps up and down.

Stop it, stop it, stop it, stop it, *stop* it.

The whistling stops. A beat of tension.
Pounding below on the ceiling.

I beg your pardon!? You bastard. I beg your —
bastard! — of all the audacity. Of all the breath-
taking — right!

He jumps harder.

There! Take that, you whistling fool! On top of
the world, are you? Well, you're still one floor
below me! Got it? One floor below me! Below me!
You cheery whistling bastard! Below — me!!

Door slams below, Doyle listens. Footsteps on
stair. They approach. Doyle listens. Knock at
door. Doyle waits. Another knock. He barks
like a big dog. Slow fade to black.

11/

Later. Knocking at the door. Doyle sits in the dark.

Afternoon. Days later. Music next door.
Doyle uses his boots to hit the floor; Remple
responds with an empty beer can.

DOYLE

Told you he was angry, Plimley. Underneath all
that high-pitched cheeriness. Just a cover, in the
end. He's as miserable as the rest of us and now
he knows it. The veneer has cracked, Remple.
Who would have guessed how easily? Stopped
puttering, too. Just sits there all day cracking his
knuckles and tossing the occasional empty beer
can at the ceiling. Waiting for my next move.
Luckily, I can hear him better than he can hear
me, not only because of my distinct auditory
advantage but because sound rises as a general
rule.

Unless, of course, it's a supplication to heaven.
Eh, Remple?

Now she's done it; dropped her precious old 78
record. That's it. Finally you've done it. Now
everything's broken.

   Another beer can.

There. Follows me around the room wherever I
go. You can't unnerve me.

Did someone say they wanted ice cream? Why is
he back?

By the way. While I was peering through the mail boxes this morning, Plimley, I couldn't help notice another rejection letter for you.

Meanwhile, over in Valerie's mailbox, a letter has arrived.

It's been so long now, that I — that I —

Not that I don't intend to go through with my plan. I have to go through with my plan.

Given the choices, I don't see what else there is.

Check myself into a loony bin? I'd have to be insane.

Anyway, once was — Especially at such a tender age. Driven mad, poor me, by the world's rasping utterances.

It's virtually impossible to be sprung from one of those psychiatric institutions, you know. If you behave badly you're a psychopath; if you behave well, you're a sociopath. So you try not to behave at all, which doesn't get you out but it does get you shock treatment. I thought that maybe if they electrocuted the shit out of my brain, it might be retrograde to my hearing. I became more atuned, not less.

Door above.

Plimley?

I'm telling the story of my life, and he goes down to collect his mail.

He approaches the ceiling and listens.

He can barely pour the booze into the glass. Now to this morning's rejection letter. Not too quickly, Plimley — please — we want to savour the moment as much as we can. The addicted gambler before he looks at the card. Only moment that's worth anything. Dear, dear. He can barely bring himself to do it. Opened the envelope, but he won't take the letter out. Fixing himself another drink. Steady.

He's pushed himself around to face the outcome from another angle. Yes; that'll improve his chances.

Rubs the rim of the glass on his bottom lip as he studies the letter.

To believe it's possible. That's the thing, eh.

Down goes the drink, gripping at his throat. That's it. Heart thumping like a pile driver. Over to the table. Pick it up. Slide the fingers in. Pull. There it is. Look at it. Crisp. Neatly, tightly folded. Listen to the play of that stationery. The quality. So fine a weave it murmurs in the fingertips. Flip it open. Intake of breath. Searching the page, now, for something, anything other than the inevitable, and then:

The slow, heavy exhalation. And that's it. Over. The letter drops.

    Beat.

Let it drop, Plimley. Go on. Accept your fate, like the rest of us. What you're hearing, Mrs. Noon, is a grown man in the throes of — I don't know what you'd call that.

He gets up on the bed and listens.

Amazing, isn't it. How weirdly ecstatic, a person can sound when actually they — they —

Pause.

Plimley?

*A shadow of deep concern crosses his brow.
Fade to black.*

13/

*Later that evening. Doyle loads his pistol,
using powder from firecrackers.*

DOYLE
Why hasn't she opened it yet?

Open it! Open it!

Sorry, Valerie. Sorry. I, really — I — shouldn't be
getting angry with you. It's just — don't open it.
Open it.

   Toying with the gun.

Nobody at the Museum even remembered me
you know; of course I only worked the two
nights. Never mind; they were long nights.

I can't believe this is actually how people used to
kill each other. At least I'll be historically —

I thought of jumping. But it would only have the
right dramatic effect if I passed your window on
the way down.

And let's be honest. The sound of a body hitting
pavement, it's really — it doesn't — resonate, exactly.

Really it was this or nothing. Go ahead and open
the letter.

   Beat.

She's opening the letter.

'My dearest neighbour, Valerie'. What a salutation. Has there ever been a more appalling letter?

Pause. She looks at the envelope. No return address. It says in the letter who I am. Just keep —

Above, a cork pops.

Listen to it. Celebrating his little victory, up there, all by himself. What could be more insipid? Local champagne. I've never heard a drier cork. It's only the battle Plimley. Wait 'til the critics sink their teeth into your pretentious little hide. Eh, Mrs. Noon?

The other wall.

Fallen over, and that's it, you see. The end, sorry to say. No. Not Harold. No one, dear. No one. You're just like one of those black beetles, tipped over on its back, wriggling its sticky little legs in the garden. Its little legs. Help me. Help me. Poor little old beetle.

Valerie's wall.

She gasps. She'll be at the part, now, where I tell her how she sounds when she sleeps. Purring like a little cat, under the whispering sheets. How I'm with her, night after night, all ears. A sentinel.

How I've come to know her daily rituals, just listening to those footsteps; the mornings of frantic hobbling about looking for a misplaced shoe. Or rushing to the rescue of some burnt toast. Or looking for her key. Or looking for her apartment.

And, of course, the sound of her tears.

It's too much. She needs to sit down.

This is the part where I despair the human condition. The inextricable self-containment of our hearts. I knew it when I saw you that afternoon. You won't remember, but in the middle of the exfoliating bit, I looked at you and said 'I love you.' Didn't just think it, no, I said it. Aloud. Looked directly into your face and out it jumped: 'I love you.' Were words ever more clear? There was a brief pause, but then you smiled, and you answered so sweetly, with such care and understanding. 'Certainly. Would like a bag for those?'

A thoughtful beat.

Was there a crueller moment, in the whole history of cosmetology?

Suddenly.

A bag for what? Yes, if you wouldn't mind wrapping those little pieces of my heart in tissue paper and stuffing them into a box, that would be —

I hurried through the department store, back out into the street. I thought — I thought — I need quiet. I need to hear myself think. The world is caving in. And there are road crews, road crews everywhere; drilling into the pavement of my brain. A graveyard.

It was so perfectly — in there — compared to everything — you know — outside. Just the sound of graves. Outside the whole idea is noise. A constant clammering. For what, I don't — daily survival. *Affirmation.* But in there, mute repose. Like dunking your head backwards in the bath. If I could have found a shovel, I would have buried myself.

> *Beat.*

Why did I ever try to reach you?

> *Going to the wall, he nervously puts the gun to his head.*

P.S. I don't expect you to come running to my door at this point; but it would be a nice surprise. Let's just say I'm hopefully pessimistic.

The main thing to realize is this, my darling Valerie, my neighbour: your search for love is utterly futile. All you ever needed to do was go out the door and turn to your right.

> *Beat*

Should I have said left?

> *From below, a loud gunshot.*

> *Blackout.*

14/

Sirens. Doyle listens at the floor.

DOYLE
They're zipping him into the bag. There you go,
Remple. Body returned; like a rented costume.

One of the cops is whistling.

Blackout.

15/

Later. Doyle listens at Valerie's wall.
Blackout.

16/

Later still. Doyle stands in the middle of the room, barely able to control his rage. Blackout.

17/

More time has passed.
He listens at the wall, empty of feeling.

DOYLE

That's the last of her things. She can't find her key, of course. All turned around. Left, right, what's the difference, eh?

Don't worry everybody. I'll be fine.

I should have guessed how sympathetic she'd be. To run next door like that, the *other* next door like that, without a second thought, in order to save someone's life. It makes me love her even more, if that's possible. With or without a sense of direction. And why did there have to be a neurotic, toilet-obsessed single man living on the other side of her? Did I mention Raskey's dermatitis? It was love at first sight. And, of course they both assumed — everyone in the building just assumed — along with the police of course, that the letter came from Mr. Remple — who conveniently *off*ed himself at the critical moment; taking credit for the suicide note. So touched was everyone, by Mr. Remple's story of *infrasonic sensitivity* — they're even doing a little piece on him in the longshoreman's newsletter. And he's become the talk of the hallways; the rage. A sort of hero of despair; piles of flowers at his door. People are so anxious to grieve these days about anything. I can't put a load of whites in the wash without hearing his tragic story, tearfully recounted, from the other side of the soap dispenser.

And now, of course, to kill myself, would just seem — oddly derivative.

Would you listen to all that gurgling over there. Good Lord. Feeding you like a baby, that woman. Changing your nappies. Is this really what you want, Mrs. Noon? A chatty careworker? Keeping you alive, inexplicably and indefinitely. Who called the Department of Health anyway?

Oh, right. Me.

He sighs. On a more optimistic note.

I'm sure Valerie wouldn't have liked me anyway. Once she really got to know me. In a horrible sort of way it all turned out for the —

She's not alone, that's the thing, eh. That's the — not alone is the thing.

Suddenly raging.

Either he's kissing her with an open mouth again, Mrs. Noon, or feeding crème brûlée to an octopus. People in love sound so — sticky. Well, they're bonding, ha, ha. I thank God they won't be living here. Thank God.

Noise from the hall; he runs up and peeks out the door.

They're closing the door behind them, finally. She's still scouring her purse. Where is it?

Where's the *key?* Wait. He's got it, Mrs. Noon.
Has symbiosis ever been more touching?

> *The door locks. He shuts the door, quickly, as*
> *the loves pass. Pause. He cries, quietly. After*
> *a moment he pulls himself together.*

Right. So who's next, I wonder.

> *Beat.*

Of the two people who've looked at the place so
far, I think I prefer the asthmatic saxophonist,
believe it or not. It's not that I have anything
against transvesticism; god knows it's the
cornerstone of the Russian Orthodox Church. It's
the sound of chest hair being ripped off in wax
strips that drives me up the wall. And, of course,
the shoes. There's only one thing worse than
having a heavy-set man in high heels living next
door to you. And that's having him live above
you.

Cream?

Speaking of which. I wonder when Plimley will
finally be moving out. Now that he's — Not that
we'll — one gets used to things, isn't it true; even
awful things. Isn't that the essence of life?
Acquiescence?

His book is already out. Can you believe it?
Remarkably fast; but then, I suppose it's so much
simpler, these days, to just go ahead and publish
everything and read it later. Look. A review.

> *With newspaper.*

'Mr. Plimley's sad, twisted chronicle' — blah,
blah. 'Set in the heartless world of' blah, blah.
'Heartless world', Mrs. Noon; now there's a —
The hero is an eccentric named *Mr. Heard.* And
the book's called *Overheard,* because the narrator
lives directly above the this crazy Mr. Heard,
'over' him, in other words; hears him ranting, day
and night, up through the — heating — duct —
isn't that clever — of all places — the —

Pause. Doyle looks up to the vent. Blackout.

18/

As in the first scene, Doyle stands in jacket,
holding a package. From this package he
produces an old 78 record.

DOYLE
> It wasn't easy, Mrs. Noon, but I found it.
>
> Shut up, would you? Harold is dead.
>
> *Now he produces Plimley's new novel.*
>
> So. This is it, is it — Plimley? Exposed. By a
> drunken member of the literary set; pardon the
> redundancy.
>
> *Calling up through the vent.*
>
> Is there no privacy left in the world?
>
> God. Listen to that care-worker. Why is it always
> the *tone deaf* who hum?
>
> *Listens.*
>
> Tucking the old girl in, are you? She'll be up and
> about anyway, but do what you must in the name
> of interminability.
>
> *Suddenly running to the wall.*
>
> And see if you can *please* turn her on her side
> before you go. The snoring is just — no.

Door.

Too late. Gone for the day. Just you and me, Mrs. Noon. And your deviated septum. Christ Almighty.

And the ice cream truck again. Another eleven hundred rounds of 'Turkey In The Straw.' Is there a worse sound? Well, only one. Behind the uproar and the traffic of daily life, is the smallest, the most terrifying, sound you could ever hope to hear. Undetectable. But if everything else in the world fell silent for a moment, you could probably just make out the whispered undertone of a large round object turning slowly, pointlessly, in space; all on its own.

He puts on the old record.

No, Mrs. Noon. Not Harold, no. Most definitely not. It's only me. Harold, as I have told you a million times, is — Harold is —

Sighs.

— is here, Mrs. Noon.

Leaning his head on the wall.

Harold is here.

The old song plays as the lights fade to black.

The End.